THE PRAYING ATHLETE
QUOTE BOOK

VOL 7

LIVING LIFE
PART 1

Unless otherwise indicated, Scripture quotations in this book are taken from The Holy Bible, *New International Version®, NIV®*. Copyright © 1973, 1978, 1984, 2011 by Biblica, Inc.™ Used by permission. All rights reserved worldwide.

Published by The Core Media Group, Inc., P.O. Box 2037, Indian Trail, NC 28079.

Cover & Interior Design: Ashlyn Helms

Printed in the United States of America.

VOL 7
LIVING LIFE
PART 1

I know the progress will be tough and maybe lonely at times as I find new friends and people to help me. But this I do know, I must make the changes in my life because I cannot survive just being ordinary, when I know I was created to be extraordinary. I will make progress everyday from now on and promise myself not to allow my past or laziness to paralyze my future. I will be this person of change. I must be the person of change. It starts now, today!

As you step out today into your new day and your new start, keep this in mind: Anything and everything that has ever been accomplished at one time or another was new. For you see the newness of each day is another start toward where you desire to go. So embrace this day beginning with a fresh dose of energy. It is just another step toward the hope that is within your soul. Keep stepping and you will arrive to the DESTINATION and GOAL of YOUR choice. Meanwhile, continue to gather, grow and challenge your talents daily.

Read more, attend church, get around people that can help me grow. Spend more time thinking about the future and mapping it out and less about what happened in the past. Find the motivation to read and listen to things that build into my person. Sleep less and exercise my brain and my physical body

**Educate = Read More
Empower = Believe More
Elevate = Achieve More**

People will try to wipe you away, discount who you are and say things that will hurt you. But stand tall and fly away to those you know care and love you.

What will you accomplish today, before the next sunrise?

You each add value into each other's lives by getting to know each other more and more, and by giving and not taking. For you see, this is not the world's love you see on TV. This is true love that can only be found by opening one's heart to another and being yourself...finding the joy in the journey together, no matter how long or hard.

You are loved when you are born. You will be loved when you die. In between, YOU have to manage!!!

We are are always in motion! The ocean moves everyday, the waves come to the shoreline 24/7. There is purpose in the ocean's motion. Does your motion have purpose? If so what is the purpose? Make your motion count everyday, just like the ocean!

In our lives, we can chase and
fill our time with the pursuit
of material things. While
doing this we can easily lose
sight of what we do have and
the Blessing of today. As you
strive for excellence always
maintain The Thankful Heart.
It will certainly project you
and give back great rewards
to you and your talents.

It is your passion that will
overtake the competition.
It is your passion that will
not allow yourself to set an
artificial ceiling of growth and
success. Your passion will take
you beyond what you thought
was possible and delete
the word impossible from
your vocabulary.
Live life with
AMAZING PASSION.

Time is of the essence.
I must maintain my focus.
My strong will has carried me.
It is about to happen.
I will chain myself daily to
purpose and passion.
I will follow my heart.
I cannot be deterred.
Doubters will soon see.
I believe.
IT WILL HAPPEN.

Sometimes we have to dig deep to take out the problems we put into our own life.

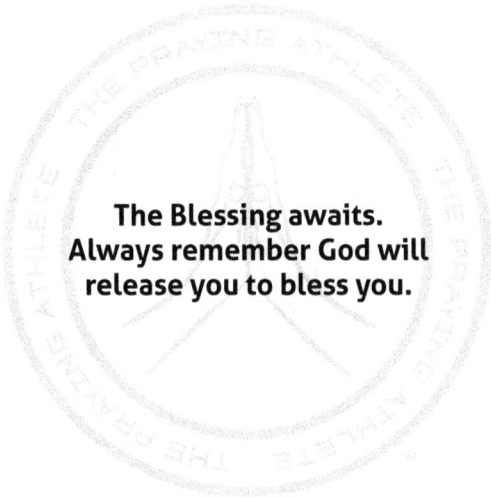

**The Blessing awaits.
Always remember God will
release you to bless you.**

Finding the wow factor in life can be as simple as releasing something to find the something that God has for you.

Where is your power coming from? Try this. Tap into the power of the one that created you. His power is endless and bountiful.

The pain of a breakup, no matter what it may be, can be intense and misunderstood. Pain is actually the first step to healing. We cannot heal if we never embrace the pain and hurt. Jesus experienced the greatest hurt and his healing was marvelous. It brought a new life and new body. So as much as it hurts, know it is better to go through the pain than to live in the pain and hurt for an entire life. The healing may seem long, but in the scope of life it is very short. So remember, the pain is actually healing masked.

Preparing for your success of tomorrow will be tougher than you think or realize. That is why only a few will make it to the other side.
Will it be you?
Do your part daily and make choices that will carry you to the other side! Know that your competition will eliminate itself. Many will lack the endurance to finish. Let that never be said of you. Go now and set out to compete daily, finish and finish strong.

Finding hope can be a
challenge in this world.
Instead of searching for the
hope you need, give hope to
others and the hope you
desire will find you at the
doorsteps of your life.

Give what you want:
Give Love, Get Love.
Give Hope, Get Hope.
Give Friendship, Get a Friend.
Give Time, Get Time.
Give Resources,
Get Resources.
Give Help, Get Help.
Give into Relationships,
Get Positive Relationships.
Give into Fitness, Get Fit.

Live your life for you, your family, and to honor God. What others think or believe is irrelevant. Once you believe this and engage in this thought, you will be free from what others do or think. Instead of saying, "Look at how much fun they are having.", you will say, "I'm glad they could that".

The freedom that comes with enjoying your minutes and seizing your time will free your spirit to enjoy life as it was meant to be. We will be simple and satisfied with ourselves, and willing to serve others rather than ourselves.

The difference between two things is called Gap. I have started something called The Gap Principal.
Here are some examples: The difference between wanting to a professional athlete and being a professional athlete, or wanting to be successful in whatever field and being successful. I call this The Gap Principal. It is what happens between the gaps that allows for success.
If we do not fill this gap, we will always stay in the want stage while life passes by.
Fill the gap if you really want it.

In this life, some will try to discourage you and say you cannot accomplish the goals and plans that are within your heart. No matter what your personal circumstances or challenges, make the adjustments.

We walk around life in a
state of paralysis because we
cannot let go of our past.
Letting go of the past is the
first step to find the hope that
is ahead. Our future cannot be
embraced if we continue to
fall and get pulled back
into the past.

Others will deplete your
dream and strip away your
belief, but be prayerful
and you can connect yourself
with people you add value
to your life. You may have to
search for that person, but
that special connection will
sustain you during the
storms of life.

Every day you must purchase perseverance, patience, honesty, endurance, truthfulness, determination and focus.

Remember on this day and everyday that you are precious and beautiful, inside and out. Once God delievers His perfect blessing, you will be forever respected and cherished than ever before.

Today choose this:
Give thanks for your job!
Give thanks for the resources
you receive from your job!
Give thanks for the health you
have to do your job!
Give thanks for the people
that make you better
at your job!

The challenges you have in your job will now be released, because you have given thanks for all things related to your job.

Sometimes, we need to
remember where we were
and the state of yesterday
to enjoy our new day.
This will push our confidence
to capture what is ahead.

THOUGHTS & REFLECTIONS

_____

_____

_____

_____

_____

_____

_____

_____

_____

_____

_____

_____

_____

_____

_____

_____

_____

_____

_____

_____

_____

_____

_____

_____

_____

_____

_____

_____

_____

_____

_____

_____

_____

_____

_____

_____

_____

_____

_____

_____

_____

_____

_____

_____

_____

_____

_____

_____

_____

_____

_____

_____

_____

_____

_____

_____

_____

_____

_____

_____

_____

_____

_____

_____

_____

_____

_____

_____

MY QUOTES

_____

_____

_____

_____

_____

_____

_____

_____

_____

_____

_____

_____

_____

_____

_____

_____

_____

_____

_____

_____

_____

_____

_____

_____

_____

_____

_____

_____

_____

_____

_____

_____

ACKNOWLEDGEMENTS

I want to acknowledge and say thank you to all those that helped with this project:

Nadia Guy
Ashlyn Helms
My Mom & Dad

All of my NFL Clients, current and former, that have encouraged me to share these words with others.

ABOUT
TPA

The Praying Athlete is a movement that creates an organic culture of prayer through an uplifting community and authentic conversation.

For more information, visit our website **www.theprayingathlete.com**.

Follow us on social media.

@ThePrayingAthlete

@Praying_Athlete

@ThePrayingAthlete

COLLECT ALL

8 VOL.

Our first volume of *The Praying Athlete Quote Book* addresses the topic of playing the game. Quotes and thoughts from Robert B. Walker, paired with Scripture from God's Word, allow readers to get a good idea about what playing a good game looks like.

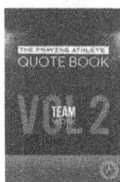

Our second volume of *The Praying Athlete Quote Book* addresses the topic of teamwork. Quotes and thoughts from Robert B. Walker, paired with Scripture from God's Word, allow readers to understand what it means to be a good teammate and surround yourself with people who lift you up.

Our third volume of *The Praying Athlete Quote Book* addresses the topic of growth & preparation for the future. Quotes and thoughts from Robert B. Walker, paired with Scripture from God's Word, allow readers to know that even though the future is uncertain, there is a plan and purpose for everyone.

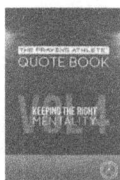

Our fourth volume of *The Praying Athlete Quote Book* addresses the topic of keeping the right mentality. Quotes and thoughts from Robert B. Walker allow readers to understand how staying in the right mindset can improve overall performance.

Our fifth volume of *The Praying Athlete Quote Book* addresses the topic of staying motivated. Quotes and thoughts from Robert B. Walker allow readers to become motivated to accomplish their goals, even when they feel they are not up to the task.

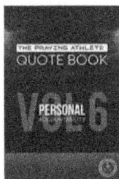

Our sixth volume of *The Praying Athlete Quote Book* addresses the topic of personal accountability. Quotes and thoughts from Robert B. Walker allow readers to think about how they can better themselves. Whether its ending a bad habit or saying no to anything that may hurt themselves or others, staying accountable will benefit one's character and performance.

Our seventh volume of *The Praying Athlete Quote Book* addresses the topic of living life. This volume is the first part in a two part living life series. Quotes and thoughts from Robert B. Walker give readers a better understanding of how to live life to the fullest.

Our eighth volume of *The Praying Athlete Quote Book* addresses the topic of living life. This volume is the second part in a two part living life series. Quotes and thoughts from Robert B. Walker give readers a better understanding of how to live life to the fullest.

FOR MORE INFO AND MERCHANDISE, PLEASE VISIT
WWW.THEPRAYINGATHLETE.COM

CHECK OUT OUR

THE PRAYING ATHLETE™
PHOTOGRAPHY
QUOTE BOOKS

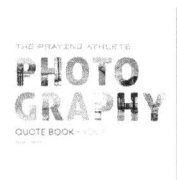

VOL. 1

VOL. 2

VOL. 3

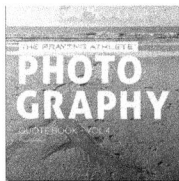

VOL. 4

*The Praying Athlete Photography Quote Book*s celebrate God's glory and magnificence through His creation. They contain photos taken by Robert B. Walker, paired with his words of wisdom, motivation, and inspiration.

www.ingramcontent.com/pod-product-compliance
Lightning Source LLC
Chambersburg PA
CBHW071746020426
42331CB00008B/2198